LONGMAN
LITERATURE
GUIDELINES

EDUCATING RITA

Willy Russell

PYGMALION

Bernard Shaw

by Theresa Sullivan

Series editors:

John Griffin
Theresa Sullivan

Introduction

I suppose the weird thing is that prior to writing *Educating Rita* I had never seen, read or heard either *Pygmalion* or indeed *My Fair Lady*. I had heard of Shaw's play and the subsequent musical but had no particular familiarity with his plot or theme. Having completed *Educating Rita* I located a copy of *Pygmalion* and spent a satisfying hour or two reading Shaw's play. As I suspected there was, for me, no similarity between the two plays other than those of plot, i.e. teacher/pupil and class divide.

Since then, of course, critics right around the world have usually mentioned *Pygmalion* in the same breath as *Educating Rita*. Does it bother me to have *Pygmalion* mentioned so often in the context of *Educating Rita*? Not one bit. To be mentioned in the same breath as the old Irish rascal Shaw is always a delight.

Willy Russell (June 1989)

This book explores the themes and issues raised in a play written in 1980, *Educating Rita* by Willy Russell, by comparing it to a play that was written in 1912, *Pygmalion* by Bernard Shaw. The two heroines, Rita and Eliza, are separated in time by sixty-eight years and in space by about 200 miles. Yet they have a great deal in common: they are both working-class girls who learn to adopt the attitudes and manners of the middle-classes with the help of a man. Shaw wrote *Pygmalion* at a time when women were fighting for the right to vote, and when the working class had very little access to education or any kind of betterment. Although Willy Russell did not write *Educating Rita* with any reference to Pygmalion, he believes, nearly seventy years later, that in spite of moves towards universal education and greater opportunities, the English class system is still strong.

It is important that you read, act through or see a production (or the films) of *Educating Rita* and *Pygmalion* before you begin the work in this book. You will be able to study the background to the plays, look carefully at the language, discuss and write about the implications of our education and class system, and improvise the plays in performance. The activities in this book offer you a chance to judge for yourself: Is the class system as strong today as it was in Eliza's time? Has the position of women in society really changed that much? What do we give up if we lose our accent and background?

Contents

The background to the plays

To understand the plays more fully, it is important to know about the different times in which each play is set. The information here and on pages 5–11 will help you to put each play in its historical setting.

Eliza Doolittle: The Edwardian Period

In 1912, the gap between rich and poor was huge. These figures show the division between them.

The total British income in 1904 was £1,710,000,000:
1.5 million rich people took £585,000,000.
3.75 million comfortable people took £245,000,000.
38 million poor people shared the remainder £880,000,000.

London flower girls.

The life of the rich

'The rich were never idle,' said J.B. Priestley ironically. Their time was taken up with a round of visits, receptions, balls, foreign visits, and sporting activities. They spent more on a single dinner than several poor families earned in a year. An Edwardian condemns their unproductive activities:

Talk, talk, talk, talk at luncheons and tea and dinner – talk at huge, undignified crowded receptions – talk at dances and at gatherings far into the night.

In the afternoons came the vital business of leaving cards and paying 'calls'. The presentation or exchange of these cards showed who was in and who was out of polite society. After three o'clock carriages and cabs carried the elite on their visits to one another. During the calls only light pleasant conversation about non-personal affairs was permitted and the visitors did not remove their outdoor clothing. Cecil Beaton remembers:

Their white kid gloves were of an immaculate quality. Over one wrist they carried a small square gold mesh bag containing a gold pencil, a handkerchief and a flat gold wallet which held their calling cards. (Cecil Beaton, *The Age of Extravagance*, 1956)

Rich people of fashion always strove to be correctly dressed, which meant changing three or four times a day. Out of doors, a lady always wore a large, highly decorated hat. She might also wear a feather boa and carry a parasol.

We were forever changing our clothes. (Lady Cynthia Asquith)

Oh those Edwardian women. All they had to do was to wear the most expensive gowns, look delightfully bored and majestically useless.

But the excesses of the rich made some uneasy. Thoughtful people such as Charles Masterman, wondered:

How long the artisans, the shop assistants, the labourers, the unemployed will be content to acquiesce in a system which expends upon a few weeks of random entertainment an amount that would support in modest comfort a decent family for a lifetime.

A shooting picnic, 1896.

Lady Jersey's garden party at Osterley Park, 1908.

Fashions for the rich, 1906.

The life of the poor

Seebohm Rowntree, a social reformer of the time was appalled by the dreadful poverty that existed:

In this land of abounding wealth, probably more than a fourth of the population are living in poverty.

Thirty per cent of the population of London was living in poverty caused by a degrading environment and the constant struggle for ill-paid work. Workers were often exhausted by fifty. Charles Booth, another reformer, writes about children:

brought up in stifling rooms, with scanty food, in the midst of births and deaths, year after year ... Their life is the life of savages ... Their food is of the coarsest description and their only luxury is drink.

The poor could only afford to buy second-hand clothes and shoes were a luxury indeed. The women dragged their skirts in the mud rather than reveal their miserable footwear. At best they wore 'boiled boots' which were picked up and patched from rubbish dumps and sold on market stalls.

Wages were very low. Maidservants earned 7s.6d. (38p) a week. Girls in East End of London factories, making corsets, brushes or umbrellas, earned 8–18s. (40p–90p) a week, not enough to buy food and clothing to keep healthy.

Yet matters had improved. By 1911, some workers were provided with pensions, sick pay and unemployment pay. This was the start of the Welfare State.

Room in a slum, 1900.

A London slum, 1903.

Children queuing for free meals in London, 1900.

Education

The 1870 Education Act meant free education for all children up to the age of twelve. Children were taught to read and write and given some historical and geographical facts. Learning was by rote and children were not encouraged to think for themselves. Although the 1870 Act was an attempt to bring a basic education to all, opportunities for the children of the poor to receive higher education were extremely limited.

Wealthy girls on a school's outing, 1900.

Working-class girls at the Modern Terrace Housewifery Centre, Greenwich, 1900.

Rita: a child of the Welfare State

Education

Rita is a child of the Welfare State. The 1944 Education Act brought great improvements in education and made schooling compulsory until the age of fifteen. In 1945, Family Allowances were introduced which enabled people to be lifted out of the poverty trap. The 1946 National Health Act brought free medical care for everyone. So Rita is healthier, better educated and better off than Eliza.

Comprehensive schools were introduced in the late 1960s and early 1970s. Before that, all children sat an exam at eleven (the 11+), on the basis of which they went to Grammar Schools, Technical High Schools, or Secondary Modern Schools. Most children went to Secondary Modern, from which very few went on to A levels or higher education. Rita would have gone to a Secondary Modern. There was a great deal of research in the 1970s to show that middle-class children were far more likely to do well at school and to go on to university than working-class children. So Rita's background put her at a disadvantage.

The Open University was set up in 1969, to give a second chance to people who had failed to get a university education through the normal channels. It has pioneered new teaching methods. Students learn in their own homes, using 'multi-media' techniques, text books and study packs, TV and radio programmes and video and audio cassettes. The course includes a week at Summer School, which provides students with an opportunity to meet each other, and to study intensively without distraction from family and job. This gives them a taste of what life as a full-time student is like. By 1975, this 'second chance' university had 50,000 students.

Comprehensive education in the 1970s.

The position of women in society

Rita has a great deal more freedom and choice than Eliza. She can vote in elections, and the advent of the pill has given her her greatest freedom. She can choose whether and when she has children and how many. Women's fashions have become far less restrictive and more practical. Modern technology has made housework much easier. And Rita can take control over her own finances, rather than accepting the will of her husband. She is also much freer, as she demonstrates, to leave her husband.

Yet many women in the 1970s, like Rita, were beginning to feel frustrated that their main roles in life were those of housewife and mother. They wanted to be treated as equals to men in law, in employment and in pay. The 1970 Equal Pay Act and the 1975 Sex Discrimination Act

helped to protect women from discrimination, but the attitudes of society needed to change before there could be real equality.

Some psychologists in the 1970s claimed that job sex-stereotyping began as early as the age of ten. Girls were persuaded to think of becoming nurses, secretaries or hairdressers rather than engineers or bricklayers. Anna Coote wrote in 1979:

Today there are still girls who grow up believing that the biggest events of their lives will be getting married and having children; they see employment as a kind of stop-gap between leaving school and finding true happiness with Mr Right. (*Equal at Work? Women in Men's Jobs*, Collins)

Your own research

▷ Make notes from either play or both, which give an impression of what each girl's life was like before she met her teacher. If you are studying both plays, set your notes out as far as possible in parallel like this:

Eliza	Rita
sells violets at a penny a bunch	works in a hairdresser's
aged 18–20	aged 26
filthy hair; dirty, muddy clothes	
single	married to Denny

Where do your notes confirm what you have read about conditions in 1912 and in 1980?

Imagine that you are the designer

▷ The designer of a play will research the historical background in order to design an appropriate set, and costumes.

1 Imagine that you are designing Eliza's clothes:
   as a flower girl;
   at Mrs Higgins' 'at home'; and
   at the ball.

   Look at the photographs on pages 4–9 and find books on costume which show the fashions of the period. Write about the costumes you would choose in as much detail as you can, and include drawings if you wish.

2 Research books of furnishings and design a set for Mrs Higgins' drawing-room. Remember that Shaw gives details of it at the beginning of Act 3 and that the room must not only reflect the period but also Mrs Higgins' character.

3 Study the photographs of Rita throughout this book and find books on fashion in the 1970s and 1980s. Design and write about what Rita would wear:
   on her first appearance (Act 1, Scene 1);
   after her visit to the Summer School (Act 2, Scene 1);
   at her last meeting with Frank (Act 2, Scene 7).

   Remember that the clothes must not only reflect the period but also Rita's character and mood. Include drawings if you wish.

Imagine that you are the director

The director must have a good understanding of the background to the play in order to create belief for the actors and for the audience.

▷ Test your own understanding. Imagine that Eliza and Rita actually meet and talk about their lives. Set their conversation out in the form of a play. If you can, try to imitate their language. (See page 19 for guidance.) Imagine that they meet before they have been transformed as a result of the influence of their teachers.

Shaw acknowledges his source story in the title he gave to his play. It is an ancient Greek legend, which the Roman poet Ovid expanded upon.

Pygmalion and Galatea

Pygmalion was a sculptor living in Cyprus in ancient times of myth and legend. He was so revolted by the wicked behaviour of the women of his time and so disgusted at their many faults that he decided to remain a bachelor and had lived for many years without a wife to share his home.

Then he carved a snowy ivory statue, marvellous for its skill and artistry. He made it lovelier than any woman ever born and fell in love with his creation. The statue had all the appearance of a real girl, so that it seemed that only modesty stopped it from coming alive and moving.

Pygmalion spent hours and days gazing at his work until he could hardly bear the passionate love that he felt. Often he ran his hands over the statue, feeling it to see whether it was flesh or ivory. He couldn't accept that ivory was all it was. He kissed the statue, and imagined that it kissed him back; he spoke to it and embraced it, and thought he felt his fingers sink into the limbs he touched, so that he was afraid that a bruise might appear where he had pressed the flesh. Sometimes he spoke flattering speeches to it and sometimes brought presents which he imagined girls would like: shells and polished pebbles, little birds and flowers of a thousand colours, and delicate jewels. He dressed the statue in women's clothes, and put rings on its fingers and long necklaces round its neck. Pearls hung from its ears and chains were looped upon its breast. Pygmalion then placed the statue on a beautiful couch, and laid its head to rest on soft pillows.

At the festival of Venus, goddess of love, when the smoke was rising from the sacrificial altar, Pygmalion stood by the altar and timidly prayed:

'If you gods can give all things, may I have as my wife – '
he did not dare say: 'The ivory maiden', but finished:
'one like the ivory maid.'

The goddess Venus heard his prayer and sent him a favourable sign: the flames at the altar rose up shooting a tongue of fire into the air.

When Pygmalion returned home, he made straight for the statue of the girl he loved, leaned over the couch, and kissed her. She seemed warm: he laid his lips on hers again and touched her shoulders. At his touch the ivory lost its hardness and grew soft. He stood amazed, afraid of being mistaken and again and again stroked the flesh gently. It was indeed a human body! The veins throbbed as he pressed them with his thumb.

At long last the girl felt his kisses and blushed. Timidly raising her eyes, she saw her lover and the light of day together. Pygmalion gave thanks to Venus for granting his wish.

Venus was present at the marriage she arranged, and nine months later, Pygmalion's bride Galatea bore a child called Paphos, and Pygmalion never regretted that his prayer was granted.

(adapted from Ovid's *Metamorphoses*)

▷ What similarities are there between Ovid's story and Shaw's play? What differences are there? Consider some of these questions in your discussion.

1 In what sense is Eliza Professor Higgins' creation?
2 Does he feel about her as Pygmalion feels about his statue?
3 If the statue starts as ivory and becomes flesh, what does Eliza start as and become? When does she actually look like the dressed up statue? What point do you think Shaw is making here?
4 Compare the characters of Pygmalion and of Higgins. Does Higgins feel gratitude? What are each man's talents?
5 Compare the endings. Should happy endings only belong to fairy stories? How are Eliza and Higgins more human and unpredictable than the characters of the legend?
6 Do you think Pygmalion is arrogant in falling in love with his own creation? Do you think Higgins is arrogant? Would it be possible to reverse the story and have a woman fall in love with a man whom she had created?
7 Both men had made the decision to stay bachelors. How do their reasons for doing so differ?
8 What does Pygmalion love about his girl? What does Higgins like or love about Eliza? Does Higgins love Eliza?
9 Do you see any similarities between this play and the story of Cinderella? Does the fairytale quality touch any characters beyond Higgins and Eliza?

▷ In the same way, decide what differences and similarities there are between Ovid's story and *Educating Rita*. Use the questions given above to help you by substituting Rita for Eliza and Frank for Higgins.

Write a fairy story

A legend or fairy story is characterised by its simple, one-dimensional characters; its simply told series of events; its limited use of dialogue; and by its shortness.

▷ Rewrite either *Educating Rita* or *Pygmalion* as a fairy story, using no more than about 500 words. This exercise will help you to grasp the essential features of the story.

▷ Compare your fairy-tale version with the original version. What have you had to leave out? What has therefore been lost?

A love story?

'I tried very hard to write a love story.'

Willy Russell

If the plays were merely vehicles for ideas, they would not hold our attention. But they contain flesh-and-blood characters who have feelings for each other. In what sense are the plays love stories? Why do both writers avoid the conventional romantic happy ending?

Higgins and Eliza

Higgins and Eliza do not have a conventionally romantic relationship. Nevertheless, as Shaw knew, audiences would want them to have a happy ending. The quarrel they have when Eliza throws the slippers at Higgins is certainly very passionate and there are indications that Higgins is perhaps dependent on her. Why might Eliza not want to marry him?

▷ Find evidence from the play which shows the nature of Higgins' and Eliza's relationship and its various stages. Use what you have found to write a piece describing their relationship.

Frank and Rita

There is no doubt that the relationship between Frank and Rita is a close one. There are indications that they are sexually attracted to each other; that they care very much for each other; that at different times they are dependent on each other; and that Frank at least suffers from sexual jealousy. Why eventually do they part?

▷ Find evidence from the play of each of these aspects of Frank and Rita's relationship and its various stages. Use what you have found to write a piece describing their relationship.

Both plays differ from the Pygmalion story in that, whereas Pygmalion lives happily-ever-after with his creation, both Higgins and Frank complain when Eliza and Rita begin to have a little life and independence of their own, and are no longer reliant on them. This extract from *Educating Rita* makes the point:

Frank Oh I've done a fine job on you, haven't I?

  Rita It's true, Frank. I can see now.

Frank You know, Rita, I think – I think that like you I shall
        change my name; from now on I shall insist upon
        being known as Mary, Mary Shelley – do you
        understand that allusion, Rita?

  Rita What?

Frank She wrote a little Gothic number called *Frankenstein*.

▷ What tone of voice do you think Frank is speaking in? What is he angry about? Why does he say 'do you understand that allusion, Rita?' How does the argument between them develop in the rest of the scene? What does Rita say which asserts her independence?

Everyone knows the name of Frankenstein, but very few know (including Rita!) that the original Frankenstein is from a novel of that name by Mary Shelley written in the early nineteenth century. Read these two extracts from the novel. The student telling the story has been studying how to create life. In the first extract, he is excited because he has discovered how to do it and is feverishly working to create life. He has great dreams for the future of renewing life in people who are dying. In the second extract, he has succeeded in animating flesh, and discovered to his horror that he has created a monster, who will eventually destroy his family.

Creating life

When I found so astonishing a power placed within my hands, I hesitated a long time concerning the manner in which I should employ it. Although I possessed the capacity of bestowing animation, yet to prepare a frame for the reception of it, with all its intricacies of fibres, muscles, and veins, still remained a work of inconceivable difficulty and labour. I doubted at first whether I should attempt the creation of a being like myself, or one of simpler organisation; but my imagination was too much exalted by my first success to permit me to doubt of my ability to give life to an animal as complex and wonderful as man. The materials at present within my command hardly appeared adequate to so arduous an undertaking; but I doubted not that I should ultimately succeed. I prepared myself for a multitude of reverses; my operations might be incessantly baffled, and at last my work be imperfect: yet, when I considered the improvement which every day takes place in science and mechanics, I was encouraged to hope my present attempts would at least lay the foundations of future success. Nor could I consider the magnitude and complexity of my plan as any argument of its impracticability. It was with these feelings that I began the creation of a human being. As the minuteness of the parts formed a great hindrance to my speed, I resolved, contrary to my first intention, to make the being of a gigantic stature; that is to say, about eight feet in height, and proportionally large. After having formed this determination, and having spent some months in successfully collecting and arranging my materials, I began.

No one can conceive the variety of feelings which bore me onwards, like a hurricane, in the first enthusiasm of success. Life and death appeared to me ideal bounds, which I should first break through, and pour a torrent of light into our dark world. A new species would bless me as its creator and source; many happy and excellent natures would owe their being to me. No father could claim the gratitude of his child so completely as I should deserve theirs. Pursuing these reflections, I thought, that if I could bestow animation upon lifeless matter, I might in process of time (although I now found it impossible) renew life where death had apparently devoted the body to curruption.

These thoughts supported my spirits, while I pursued my undertaking with unremitting ardour. My cheek had grown pale with study, and my person had become emaciated with confinement. Sometimes, on the very brink of certainty, I failed; yet I clung to the hope which the next day or the next hour might realise.

The monster wakes up

It was on a dreary night of November that I beheld the accomplishment of my toils. With an anxiety that almost amounted to agony, I collected the instruments of life around me, that I might infuse a spark of being into the lifeless thing that lay at my feet. It was already one in the morning; the rain pattered dismally against the panes, and my candle was nearly burnt out, when, by the glimmer of the half-extinguished light, I saw the dull yellow eye of the creature open; it breathed hard, and a convulsive motion agitated its limbs.

How can I describe my emotions at this catastrophe, or how delineate the wretch whom with such infinite pains and care I had endeavoured to form? His limbs were in proportion, and I had selected his features as beautiful. Beautiful! – Great God! His yellow skin scarcely covered the work of muscles and arteries beneath; his hair was of a lustrous black, and flowing; his teeth of a pearly whiteness; but these luxuriances only formed a more horrid contrast with his watery eyes, that seemed almost of the same colour as the dun white sockets in which they were set, his shrivelled complexion and straight black lips ...

I had worked hard for nearly two years, for the sole purpose of infusing life into an inanimate body. For this I had deprived myself of rest and health. I had desired it with an ardour that far exceeded moderation; but now that I had finished, the beauty of the dream vanished, and breathless horror and disgust filled my heart. Unable to endure the aspect of the being I had created, I rushed out of the room, and continued a long time traversing my bedchamber, unable to compose my mind to sleep. At length lassitude succeeded to the tumult I had before endured; and I threw myself on the bed in my clothes, endeavouring to seek a few moments of forgetfulness. But it was in vain: I slept, indeed, but I was disturbed by the wildest dreams ...

I thought that I held the corpse of my dead mother in my arms; a shroud enveloped her form, and I saw the graveworms crawling in the folds of the flannel. I started from my sleep with horror; a cold dew covered my forehead, my teeth chattered, and every limb became convulsed: when, by the dim and yellow light of the moon, as it forced its way through the window shutters, I beheld the wretch – the miserable monster whom I had created. He held up the curtain of the bed; and his eyes, if eyes they may be called, were fixed on me. His jaws opened, and he muttered some inarticulate sounds, while a grin wrinkled his cheeks. He might have spoken, but I did not hear; one hand was stretched out, seemingly to detain me, but I escaped, and rushed down stairs. I took refuge in the courtyard belonging to the house which I inhabited; where I remained during the rest of the night, walking up and down in the greatest agitation, listening attentively, catching and fearing each sound as if it were to announce the approach of the demoniacal corpse to which I had so miserably given life.

▷ After reading the extracts from *Frankenstein*, discuss the following points.

1 To what extent do Higgins and Frank share the student's feelings during the process of creation and afterwards? How many stories and films do you know that are based on the idea of someone making a great discovery or making something new only for it to result in disaster for the creator? Why do you think this theme is so popular?

2 In what ways do Higgins and Frank behave as fathers to Eliza and Rita? In what ways if any, are the women like daughters?

3 Is it a necessary part of that relationship that the 'child' – at least temporarily – rejects the 'father'?

4 Do you agree that the roles reverse in both plays so that in the end it is the men who are dependent upon the women? In what ways is each man dependent?

5 Compare Higgins' attitude to Eliza with that of Doolittle, her actual father in the play.

▷ Imagine that Higgins or Frank keep a diary. Write *either* Higgins' *or* Frank's entry when he is excited by what he is achieving, and then write the entry when he realises that his creation is no longer dependent upon him and refuses to accept his control any longer.

The language of the plays

Actresses playing either Eliza or Rita must be able to speak a cockney or Liverpudlian accent. Shaw very quickly gave up representing Eliza's speech as it sounds rather than as it is spelt because he knew that readers would find it difficult.

▷ In pairs, read aloud these examples from the characters' speech and decide where each departs from standard English. Listen to the rhythm and again decide what makes each dialect unique. (Comparing their language with that of Frank and Professor Higgins may make the differences more obvious to you.)

Rita

This was the pornography of its day, wasn't it?

It's sort of like *Men Only*, isn't it?

I didn't ask y' if it was beautiful.

Here d' y' want one?

I hate smokin' on me own. An' everyone seems to have packed up these days.

It's dead good.

Y' wanna be careful with that stuff.

Ta. I'll look after it. If I pack the course in I'll post it to y'.

There's loads I don't know.

Eliza

Oh, we are proud! He ain't above giving lesson, not him.

I'm come to have lessons, I am.

Well, if you was a gentleman, you might ask me to sit down, I think.

But they won't take me unless I can talk more genteel.

You'd had a drop in, hadn't you?

Don't mind if I do.

Oh, you are real good.

Ah-ah-ah-ah-ow-ow-oo-oo!!! I ain't dirty: I washed my face and hands afore I come, I did.

Accent and class

As Trish says there is not a lot of point in discussing beautiful literature in an ugly voice. (Rita)

It is impossible for an Englishman to open his mouth without making some other Englishman despise him. (Shaw)

Shaw has Eliza speak standard English as a result of her education with Professor Higgins, whereas Rita continues to speak with a Liverpudlian accent after her Open University Education. Do you think this indicates a change of attitude towards accents between 1912 and 1980?

▷ Look at the two quotations above. How far would you agree with them? What is meant by 'speaking correctly'? How important do you think it is to speak correctly? Is this the same as or different from speaking with an accent? Is it important to be able to change your style of speaking according to the circumstances in which you are speaking? Is what you say more important than how you say it?

Higgins says to his mother:

You have no idea how frightfully interesting it is to take a human being and change her into a quite different human being by creating a new speech for her. It's filling up the deepest gulf that separates class from class and soul from soul.

▷ Do you agree with Higgins? Is it only speech which creates the gulf that separates class from class? How does Eliza's father gain entry to the middle class? What would Willy Russell say also separates class from class?

Eliza and Rita as flesh and blood creatures

The object of Pymalion's desire is completely passive, even when she comes alive. But both Rita and Eliza are lively women with a good deal of spirit and individuality. Their men are not complete masters of the situation as Pygmalion is.

'Do you get a lot of students like me?'

Read this extract from the first scene of *Educating Rita*. Rita is by no means a passive admirer of Frank's wisdom.

Rita (*noticing the picture*) That's a nice picture, isn't it? (*She goes up to it*)

Frank Erm – yes, I suppose it is – nice ...

Rita (*studying the picture*) It's very erotic.

Frank (*looking up*) Actually I don't think I've looked at it for about ten years, but yes, I suppose it is.

Rita There's no suppose about it. Look at those tits. (*He coughs and goes back to looking for the admission paper*) Is it supposed to be erotic? I mean when he painted it do y' think he wanted to turn people on?

Frank Erm – probably.

Rita I'll bet he did y' know. Y' don't paint pictures like that just so that people can admire the brush strokes, do y'?

Frank (*giving a short laugh*) No – no – you're probably right.

Rita This was the pornography of its day, wasn't it? It's sort of like *Men Only*, isn't it? But in those days they had to pretend it wasn't erotic so they made it religious, didn't they? Do *you* think it's erotic?

Frank (*taking a look*) I think it's very beautiful.

Rita I didn't ask y' if it was beautiful.

Frank But the term 'beautiful' covers the many feelings I have about that picture, including the feeling that, yes, it is erotic.

Rita (*coming back to the desk*) D' y' get a lot like me?

Frank Pardon?

Rita Do you get a lot of students like me?

▷ Make a list of Rita's remarks which shows she is taking the lead in the conversation and that she is confident and self-assured whereas Frank is not. What remarks show that she is witty and has a mind of her own? How much of her confidence do you think is adopted for the occasion?

'I'm come to have lessons, I am.'

Read this extract from *Pygmalion* in which Eliza asks Professor Higgins for lessons.

Higgins (*brusquely, recognizing her with unconcealed disappointment, and at once, babylike, making an intolerable grievance of it*) Why, this is the girl I jotted down last night. She's no use: I've got all the records I want of the Lisson Grove lingo; and I'm not going to waste another cylinder on it. (*To the girl*) Be off with you: I don't want you.

The Flower Girl Don't you be so saucy. You ain't heard what I come for yet. (*To Mrs Pearce, who is waiting at the door for further instructions*) Did you tell him I come in a taxi?

Mrs Pearce Nonsense, girl! What do you think a gentleman like Mr Higgins cares what you came in?

The Flower Girl Oh, we are proud! He ain't above giving lessons, not him: I heard him say so. Well, I ain't come here to ask for any compliment; and if my money's not good enough I can go elsewhere.

Higgins Good enough for what?

The Flower Girl Good enough for yə-oo. Now you know, don't you? I'm come to have lessons, I am. And to pay for em tə-oo: make no mistake.

Higgins (*stupent*) Well!!! (*Recovering his breath with a gasp*) What do you expect me to say to you?

The Flower Girl Well, if you was a gentleman, you might ask me to sit down, I think. Don't I tell you I'm bringing you business?

Higgins Pickering: shall we ask this baggage to sit down, or shall we throw her out of the window?

The Flower Girl (*running away in terror to the piano, where she turns at bay*) Ah-ah-oh-ow-ow-ow-oo! (*Wounded and whimpering*) I won't be called a baggage when I've offered to pay like any lady.
Motionless, the two men stare at her from the other side of the room, amazed.

▷ Make a list of Eliza's remarks which shows that she refuses to be put down. Compare Eliza's and Rita's characters as revealed in these extracts. In what ways are they similar? Dissimilar? Is there any indication that the class gap has narrowed in seventy years?

'I can do things on me own more now.'

Read these extracts. How do they show that the women have learnt their lessons and are asserting their independence?

The lights come up on Frank who is sitting at his desk marking an essay. Occasionally he makes a tutting sound and scribbles something. There is a knock at the door.

Frank   Come in.

Rita enters, closes the door, goes to the desk and dumps her bag on it. She takes her chair and places it next to Frank and sits down.

Rita   (*talking in a peculiar voice*) Hello, Frank.

Frank   (*without looking up*) Hello. Rita, you're late.

Rita   I know, Frank. I'm terribly sorry. It was unavoidable.

Frank   (*looking up*) Was it really? What's wrong with your voice?

Rita   Nothing is wrong with it, Frank. I have merely decided to talk properly. As Trish says there is not a lot of point in discussing beautiful literature in an ugly voice.

Frank   You haven't got an ugly voice; at least you *didn't* have. Talk properly.

Rita   I am talking properly. I have to practise constantly, in everyday situations.

Frank   You mean you're going to talk like that for the rest of this tutorial?

Rita   Trish says that no matter how difficult I may find it I must persevere.

Frank   Well will you kindly tell Trish that I am not giving a tutorial to a Dalek?

Rita   I am not a Dalek.

Frank   (*appealingly*) Rita, stop it!

Rita   But Frank, I have to persevere in order that I shall.

Frank   Rita! Just be yourself.

Rita   (*reverting to her normal voice*) I am being myself. (*She gets up and moves the chair back to its usual place*)

Frank   What's that?

Rita   What?

Frank   On your back.

Rita   (*reaching up*) Oh – it's grass.

Frank   Grass?

Rita   Yeh, I got here early today. I started talking to some students down on the lawn. (*She sits in her usual chair*)

Frank   You were talking to students – down there?

Rita   (*laughing*) Don't sound so surprised. I can talk now y' know, Frank.

Frank   I'm not surprised. Well! You used to be quite wary of them didn't you?

Rita   God knows why. For students they don't half come out with some rubbish y' know.

Frank   You're telling me?

Liza Oh! if I only could go back to my flower basket! I should be independent of both you and father and all the world! Why did you take my independence from me? Why did I give it up? I'm a slave now, for all my fine clothes.

Higgins Not a bit. I'll adopt you as my daughter and settle money on you if you like. Or would you rather marry Pickering?

Liza (*looking fiercely round at him*) I wouldn't marry you if you asked me; and you're nearer my age than what he is.

Higgins (*gently*) Than he is: not "than what he is."

Liza (*losing her temper and rising*) I'll talk as I like. You're not my teacher now.

Higgins (*reflectively*) I don't suppose Pickering would, though. He's as confirmed an old bachelor as I am.

Liza That's not what I want; and don't you think it. I've always had chaps enough wanting me that way. Freddy Hill writes to me twice and three times a day, sheets and sheets.

Higgins (*disagreeably surprised*) Damn his impudence! (*He recoils and finds himself sitting on his heels*).

Liza He has a right to if he likes, poor lad. And he does love me.

Higgins (*getting off the ottoman*) You have no right to encourage him.

Liza Every girl has a right to be loved.

Higgins What! By fools like that?

Liza Freddy's not a fool. And if he's weak and poor and wants me, maybe he'd make me happier than my betters that bully me and don't want me.

Higgins Can he make anything of you? That's the point.

Liza Perhaps I could make something of him. But I never thought of us making anything of one another; and you never think of anything else. I only want to be natural.

Higgins In short, you want me to be as infatuated about you as Freddy? Is that it?

Liza No I don't. That's not the sort of feeling I want from you. And don't you be too sure of yourself or of me. I could have been a bad girl if I'd liked. I've seen more of some things than you, for all your learning. Girls like me can drag gentlemen down to make love to them easy enough. And they wish each other dead the next minute.

▷ How are the characters of Eliza and Rita similar? How are they different? Compare the two sets of extracts (pages 20–21). How have the women changed? What evidence is there in the earlier extracts which would lead you to suppose that the women would behave as they do later? What change is there in their use of language? Compare and contrast the men's attitude to the women they have created.

▷ Imagine that *either* the women *or* the men meet and compare notes on the conversation they have had, in which the women assert their independence. Draw your material from the whole scene from which the extracts are taken.

Use these questions to help you write about their meeting.

What are the women trying to tell the men? What do they feel about their positions? What do they see as the advantages and disadvantages of their present position? How do they see their future? What are their feelings about the men? How do these differ from what they felt earlier on? What do the men feel about what the women tell them? Do they learn anything about themselves or the women? Would they admit to learning anything? What do they think is their relationship with the women now?

Self-betterment is a theme common to both plays. Both Eliza and Rita find out that self-improvement can bring as many problems as it solves. Study these quotations from both plays on education and self-improvement. What impression do they leave you with? Discuss the questions that follow each quotation. Find more quotations yourself on the same theme.

'I wanted a better way of livin' me life.'

Rita It's like y' sit there, don't y', watching the ballet or the opera on the telly an' – an' y' call it rubbish cos that's what it looks like. Cos y' don't understand. So y' switch it off an' say, that's fucking rubbish.

▷ Do you think people do dismiss things as rubbish because they don't understand them? Do you know of any examples? Do tastes change anyway with age, for instance? Do small children dislike what you like and vice-versa?

Rita I tried to explain to him that I wanted a better way of livin' me life. An' he listened to me. But he didn't understand because when I'd finished he said he agreed with me and that we should start savin' the money to move off our estate an' get a house out in Formby.

▷ What does Denny mean by a 'better way of living'? How has he completely misunderstood Rita?

Rita Nah, they tried their best I suppose, always tellin' us we stood more of a chance if we studied. But studyin' was just for the wimps, wasn't it? See, if I'd started takin' school seriously I would have had to become different from me mates, an' that's not allowed.

▷ Do you think that what Rita says is true? Why is studying seen as what the 'wimps' do?

Rita . . . Till, one day, y' own up to yourself an' y' say, is this it? Is this the absolute maximum I can expect from this living lark? An' that's the big moment that one, that's the point when y' have to decide whether it's gonna be another change of dress or a change in yourself.

▷ What do you expect from 'this living lark'? Do you think Rita is going the right way about achieving the maximum she can from life?

Rita . . . an' I saw this fantastic bird, all coloured it was, like dead out of place round our way. I was just gonna shout an' tell Miss but this kid next to me said, 'Keep your mouth shut or she'll make us write an essay on it.'
Frank (*sighing*) Yes, that's what we do, Rita; we call it education.

▷ This is a very cynical view of education. Is it your view? Your experience? How do you think the teacher should react if Rita had told her about the bird? What should young people gain from education?

Rita Why didn't y' just tell me, right from the start?
Frank I could have told you; but you'll have a much better understanding of something if you discover it in your own terms.

▷ Should teachers tell you what you want to know or help you to find it out for yourself?

Rita . . . I'm a freak. I can't talk to the people I live with anymore. An' I can't talk to the likes of them on Saturday, or them out there, because I can't learn the language. I'm a half-caste.

▷ Rita is discovering the problems of being an educated working-class women. Do you think her feeling of isolation is inevitable? What advice would you give her?

Frank . . . I don't know that I want to teach you. What you already have is valuable.
Rita Valuable? What's valuable? The only thing I value is here, comin' here once a week.
Frank But, don't you see, if you're going to write this sort of thing – (*he indicates the pile of essays*) – to pass examinations, you're going to have to suppress, perhaps abandon your uniqueness.

▷ What does Frank mean? What is Willy Russell criticising about examinations and education? Do you think exams are an essential part of education? Or do you think they hinder education?

Frank (*shrugging*) What I'm saying is that it's up to the minute, quite acceptable, trendy stuff about Blake; but there's nothing of you in there.

▷ Again, what is Willy Russell criticising about modern education? Do you agree with him?

  Rita I've got a room full of books. I know what clothes to wear, what wine to buy, what plays to see, what papers and books to read. I can do without you.

▷ Do you agree with Rita that she is now 'educated'. Has she done more than change her dress?

  Rita I came to tell you you're a good teacher.

▷ Do you think Frank is a good teacher? Or do you agree with his own opinion of himself?

  Rita ... I had a choice. I chose, me. Because of what you'd given me I had a choice.

▷ Do you think education gives freedom of choice? Rita obtains a good degree. Do you think that is useful in itself, regardless of what she has attained from the course?

'I am a child in your country.'

  Liza How do I know whether you took me down right? You just shew me what you've wrote about me. What's that? That ain't proper writing. I can't read that.

▷ People who can barely read and write are very much in awe of the power of words. How does Liza show here that she cannot read very well?

  Higgins This is an age of upstarts. Men begin in Kentish Town with £80 a year, and end in Park Lane with a hundred thousand. They want to drop Kentish Town; but they give themselves away every time they open their mouths.

▷ What point is Higgins making about class movement? Do you think what he is saying is still true today?

  Higgins A woman who utters such depressing and disgusting sounds has no right to be anywhere – no right to live. Remember that you are a human being with a soul and the divine gift of articulate speech.

▷ Speech distinguishes us from animals. What is Higgins implying therefore about Liza? Do we have a responsibility to make ourselves as articulate as possible?

  Pickering What about the ambassador's garden party? I'll say you're the *greatest teacher alive* if you make that good.
  Higgins Yes: in six months – in three if she has a good ear and a quick tongue – I'll take her anywhere and pass her off as anything.

▷ Do you think Higgins shows himself to be a good teacher? Is it important to learning to have a good student as well as a good teacher? Is the difference between a duchess and a flower girl merely a matter of speech?

Mrs Higgins You certainly are a pretty pair of babies, playing with your live doll.

Higgins Playing! The hardest job I ever tackled. make no mistake about that, mother. But you have no idea how frightfully interesting it is to take a human being and change her into a quite different human being by creating a new speech for her. It's filling up the deepest gulf that separates class from class and soul from soul.

▷ Do you think Higgins is an irresponsible teacher? Has Eliza changed her class by changing her speech?

Mrs Higgins . . . the problem of what is to be done with her afterwards.

Higgins I don't see anything in that. She can go her own way, with all the advantages I have given her.

▷ What advantage will Eliza still not have, which is essential if she is to live as a lady?

Liza What am I fit for? What have you left me fit for? Where am I to go? What am I to do? What's to become of me?

▷ Do you think Eliza is better or worse off than before she met Higgins?

Higgins You will jolly soon see whether she has an idea that I haven't put into her head or a word that I haven't put into her mouth.

▷ Is this true of Eliza? Does it remind you of anything in *Educating Rita*?

Liza … the difference between a lady and a flower girl is not how she behaves, but how she's treated.

▷ What does Eliza mean? Do you think what she says is true? What does this say about class attitudes?

Liza I am a child in your country.

▷ Does this remind you of anything that Rita says? What do their situations have in common?

Higgins The great secret, Eliza, is not having bad manners or good manners or any other particular sort of manners, but having the same manner for all human souls.

▷ What does this reveal about Shaw's views about class?

Liza Why did you take my independence from me? Why did I give it up? I'm a slave now, for all my fine clothes.

▷ How is this different from what Rita feels at the end of her play? Do you think Eliza has achieved independence or not in the end?

The portrayal of education

▷ You are now in a position to write a piece about the portrayal of education and class in either *Educating Rita* or *Pygmalion* or both.

1 Collect the points you made in your discussion and present them in a logical order. What finally do Russell and Shaw say about the nature of education, its influence, and its place in the British class structure?

2 Imagine that either Rita and Frank or Eliza and Mrs Higgins talk about their teacher-pupil relationship many years later. Invent the conversation they might have, as they look back on events, and show each one's attitude to the process of education.

3 What class differences still exist in terms of:
leisure pursuits,
choice of children's names,
cars,
holidays,
clothes,
houses and furnishings?

Make a list and then write a piece to show how far you think the class system has changed – or not changed – since Eliza's time.

What happens next?

Both plays end ambiguously. Higgins does not accept that Eliza will marry Freddy and never come back. Rita refuses to go to Australia with Frank but cuts his hair as a friendly gesture. Have the women become too independent to need their men? Why should Eliza think of marrying Freddy?

Should Eliza marry Higgins?

▷ Read Shaw's account of why Eliza would not or should not marry Higgins.

... People in all directions have assumed, for no other reason than that she [Eliza] became the heroine of a romance, that she must have married the hero of it. This is unbearable, not only because her little drama, if acted on such a thoughtless assumption, must be spoiled, but because the true sequel is patent to anyone with a sense of human nature in general, and of feminine instinct in particular.

Eliza, in telling Higgins she would not marry him if he asked her, was not coquetting: she was announcing a well-considered decision. When a bachelor interests, and dominates, and teaches, and becomes important to a spinster, as Higgins with Eliza, she always, if she has character enough to be capable of it, considers very seriously indeed whether she will play for becoming that bachelor's wife, especially if he is so little interested in marriage that a determined and devoted woman might capture him if she set herself resolutely to do it. Her decision will depend a good deal on whether she is really free to choose; and that, again, will depend on her age and income. If she is at the end of her youth, and has no security for her livelihood, she will marry him because she must marry anybody who will provide for her. But at Eliza's age a good-looking girl does not feel that pressure; she feels free to pick and choose. She is therefore guided by her instinct in the matter. Eliza's instinct tells her not to marry Higgins. It does not tell her to give him up. It is not in the slightest doubt as to his remaining one of the strongest personal interests in her life. It would be very sorely strained if there was another woman likely to supplant her with him. But as she feels sure of him on that last point, she has no doubt at all as to her course, and would not have any, even if the difference of twenty years in age, which seems so great to youth, did not exist between them.

▷ Do you agree with Shaw? What are the limitations faced by women at this time? What choices does Rita have that would not have been possible for Eliza? Do you think that Rita will see Frank, or that Eliza will see Higgins, again?

▷ Write an additional scene which occurs two years later in which *either* Rita is talking to Frank *or* Eliza to Higgins. What are their lives like now? What do they talk about? Will they talk about the past?

George Bernard Shaw (1856–1950). Shaw was a dramatist, critic and social thinker. As a socialist, he was firmly convinced of the emancipating value of genuine education, although the price of achieving it could be high.

Mrs Joe Bradshaw in Willy Russell's play *Shirley Valentine* is what Rita would have been in twenty years' time if she hadn't tried to break free of the limitations of her life. Mrs Bradshaw is a 42-year-old mother of two grown-up children. Her self-confidence and sense of her own worth are broken by school, marriage and life. She is reduced to talking to the kitchen wall whilst preparing her husband's evening meal, which must be on the table when he comes in at night. But her former self before her marriage – Shirley Valentine – is longing to get out. Her feminist friend offers a holiday to Greece, and Shirley at last seizes the opportunity to escape out of the mould society has cast for her. There is only one character in the play – Shirley. This extract is taken from near the beginning of the play.

Shirley

Oh God, look at the time. What am I doin' sittin' here talkin' and *he*'ll be in for his tea, won't he. An' what's he like? My feller. What's he like, wall? Well, he likes everything to be as it's always been. Like his tea always has to be on the table as he comes through that door. If the plate isn't landin' on the mat, there's ructions. I've given up arguin'. I said to him, once, I said, "Listen, Joe. If your tea isn't on the table at the same time every night it doesn't mean that the pound's collapsed y' know, or that there's been a world disaster. All it means, Joe, is that one of the billions of human bein's on this planet has to eat his tea at a different time." Well, did it do any good? I could've been talkin' to that. Couldn't I, wall?

Pause

I always said I'd leave him when the kids grew up. But by the time they'd grown up there was nowhere to go. Well, you don't start again at forty-two, do y'? They say, don't they, they say once you've reached your forties life gets a bit jaded an' y' start to believe that the only good things are things in the past. Well, I must have been an early developer, I felt like that at twenty-five. I'm not sayin' he's bad, my feller. He's just no bleedin' good. Mind you, I think most of them are the same, aren't they? I mean they're lovely at first. Know, when they're courtin' y'. Y' know, before you've had the horizontal party with them, oh they're marvellous then. They'll do anything for y'. Nothin' is too much trouble. But the minute, the very minute, after they've first had y' – their behaviour starts to change. It's like that advert, isn't it? I was watchin' it the other night – y' know, Milk Tray Man. Oh, he's marvellous, isn't he? Y' see him, he dives off a thousand foot cliff an' swims across two miles of water, just to drop off a box of chocolates. An' y' learn from that that the lady loves Milk Tray. And that the lady's been keepin' her legs firmly closed. Because if she hadn't, if he'd had his way with her he wouldn't go there by divin' off a thousand foot cliff an' swimmin' through a ragin' torrent. He'd go by bus. An' there'd be no chocolates. If she mentioned the chocolates that he used to bring he'd say "Oh no. I've stopped bringin' y' chocolates, babe, 'cos y' puttin' a bit too much weight on." D' y' know, when y' think about it, Cadbury's could go out of business if women didn't hold back a bit. I don't hate men. I'm not a feminist. Not like Jane. Jane's my mate. Now, she's a feminist. Well, she likes to think she is, y' know she reads *Cosmopolitan* an' says that all men are

potential rapists. Even the Pope. Well, Jane does hate men. She divorced her husband, y' know. I never knew him, it was before I met Jane. Apparently she came back from work one mornin' an' found her husband in bed with the milkman. With the milkman, honest to God! Well, apparently, from that day forward Jane was a feminist. An' I've noticed, she never takes milk in her tea. I haven't known Jane all that long, but she's great. She's goin' to Greece for a fortnight. Next month she's goin'. God, what will I do for two weeks? She's the only one who keeps me sane. Jane's the only one I ever talk to, apart from the wall – isn't she, wall? She is, I said to her this mornin', "Jane, I won't half miss y'." You know what she said to me? "I want you to come with me."

She laughs

Silly bitch. Hey, wall, wall, imagine the face on "him". Imagine the face if he had to look after himself for two weeks. Jesus, if I go to the bathroom for five minutes he thinks I've been hijacked.

▷ What similarities are there with the character of Rita? What differences are there? (Consider such things as lifestyle, use of language and rhythm, sense of humour.)

The second extract is from towards the end of the play when Shirley has gone to Greece and met a Greek waiter, who, although she knows it's just a short-term romance, treats her with consideration and concern, and makes her feel she is an individual with a sense of her own worth. She decides to stay and live and work on her Greek island.

Well I'm sittin' there an' he came out to serve me. "Erm, excuse me," I said to him, "I know this sounds a bit soft but would you mind ... I mean would you object if I moved this table an' chair over there, by the edge of the sea?" Well, he looked at me for a minute. "You want," he said, "you want move table and chair to the sea? What for? You don't like here at my bar?" "Oh yeh," I said, "yeh, it's a lovely bar but – but I've just got this soft little dream about sittin' at a table by the sea." "Ah," he said, an' he smiled. "A dream, a dream. We move this table to the edge of the sea, it make your dream come true?" "Erm, yeh," I said. "I think so." "Then, is no problem. I move the table for you. And tonight when I serve in my bar, I say to customer – 'tonight, tonight I make someone's dream come true'." Well, I thought for a second he was bein' sarcastic – 'cos in England it would have been. But no, he carries the table an' chair over here an' he brings me out this glass of wine I've ordered. Well, I paid him an' thanked him but he said to me, "No, I thank you. Enjoy your dream", then he gave a little bow an' he was gone, back to the taverna, leavin' me alone with the sea an' the sky an' me soft little dream. Well, it's funny, isn't it, but y' know if you've pictured somethin', y' know, if you've imagined how somethin's gonna be, made a picture of it in your mind, well it never works out, does it? I mean for weeks I'd had this picture of meself, sittin' here, sittin' here drinkin' wine by the sea; I even knew exactly how I was gonna feel. But when it got to it, it wasn't a bit like that. Because when it got to it, I didn't feel at all lovely an' serene. I felt pretty daft actually. A bit stupid an' – an' awfully, awfully old. What I kept thinkin' about was how I'd lived such a little life. An' one way or another even that would be over pretty soon. I thought to meself, my life has been a crime really – a crime against God, because ... I didn't live it fully. I'd allowed myself to live this little life when inside me there was so much. So much more that I could have lived a bigger life with – but it had all gone unused, an' now it never would be. Why – why do y' get ... all this life, when it can't be used? Why – why do y' get ... all these ... feelin's an' dreams an' hopes if they can't ever be used. That's where Shirley Valentine disappeared to. She got lost in all this unused life. An' that's what I was thinkin', sittin' there on me own, starin' out at the sea, me eyes open wide an' big tears splashin' down from them. I must've sat there for ages because the noise from the hotel bar had died away an' even the feller from the taverna was lockin' up for the night. He came to collect me glass. It was still full. I hadn't even taken a sip. He saw that I was cryin' but he didn't say anythin'. He just sat down, on the sand an' stared out at the sea. An' when I'd got over it, when it was all right to talk, he said, "Dreams are never in the places we expect them to be." I just smiled at him. "Come," he said, "I escort you back to your hotel." An' he did. An' he told me his name was Costas an' I told him my name was Shirley ...

I'd fallen in love with him. I'd fallen in love with the idea of livin'. An' every day, when I woke up, when I came down here with Jane, when we went an' had a coffee or a drink at Costas's taverna, when I was lyin' in me bed, just droppin' off to sleep, it was always there in me head – this shocking thought – "I'm not goin' back. I'm not goin' back."

Pause

An', of course, all the time I knew really. I knew I'd have to go back in the end. I knew that I was just one of millions before me who'd gone on a holiday an' had such a

good time that they didn't want to go home. Because we don't do what we want to do. We do what we have to do. An' pretend it's what we want to do. An' what I wanted to do was to stay here and be Shirley Valentine. An' what I had to do was to go back there, back to bein' St Joan of the Fitted Units. An' all through the days, an' when I said goodbye to Costas, an' on the way to the airport, an' in the long queue for the check-in desk, I didn't know if I'd do what I wanted to do, or what I had to do. We were standin' there, in this queue, me an' Jane an' all the others who had to go back. An' I remembered this question I was gonna ask Jane. So I said to her, "Jane, Jane, why is it that there's all this unused life?"

'All this unused life'

▷ Shirley talks of how she 'got lost in all this unused life.' A little later she says: 'An' most of us die ... long before we're dead. An' what kills us is the terrible weight of all this unused life that we carry around.' How much do you think this is a theme of *Educating Rita* and *Shirley Valentine*?

Read this extract from Willy Russell's account of his own schooling.

When I was eleven they sent me to a secondary school in Huyton. Like all the other Knowsley kids I was frightened of Huyton. There were millions of new houses there and flats, and everyone said there were gangs with bike chains and broken bottles and truck spanners. What everyone said was right; playtime was nothing to do with play, it was about survival. Thugs roamed the concrete and casually destroyed anything that couldn't move fast enough. Dinner time was the same only four times as long.

If you were lucky enough to survive the food itself you then had to get out into the playground world of protection rackets, tobacco hustlers, trainee contract killers and plain no-nonsense sadists. And that's without the teachers!

... We even had a long lesson every week called 'silent reading'; just enter the classroom and pick up a book, start reading and as long as you made no noise you were left completely alone with your book. I remember clearly, during one of these lessons, locked into a novel, the sun streaming through the windows, experiencing the feeling of total peace and security and thinking what a great thing it must be to write books and create in people the sort of feeling the author had created in me. I wanted to be a writer!

It was a wonderful and terrible thought – wonderful because I sensed, I knew, it was the only thing for me. Terrible because how could I, a kid from the 'D' stream, a piece of factory fodder, ever change the course that my life was already set upon? How the hell could I ever be the sort of person who could become a writer? It was a shocking and ludicrous thought, one that I hid deep in myself for years, but one that would not go away.

During my last year at school they took us to a bottle-making factory in St Helens, me and all the other kids who were obviously factory types. I could feel the brutality of the place even before I entered its windowless walls. Inside, the din and the smell were overpowering. Human beings worked in there but the figures I saw, feeding huge and relentlessly hungry machines, seemed not to be a part of humanity but a part of the machinery itself. Those men who were fortunate enough to not have to work directly with the machinery, the supervisors, foremen I suppose, glared, prodded, occasionally shouted. Each one of them looked like Anders from the metal-work class.

Most of the kids with whom I visited that place accepted that it was their lot to end up in that place. Some even talked of the money they would earn and made out that they couldn't wait to get inside those walls.

But, in truth, I think they all dreaded it as much as I. Back in school I stared at the geography books I hadn't read, the history pages and science I hadn't studied, the maths books (which would still be a mystery today, even if I'd studied them from birth), and I realized that with only six months' schooling to go, I'd left it all hopelessly too late. Like it or not I'd end up in a factory.

▷ Does the extract give you a sense of why Willy Russell is concerned with 'unused life'? In what ways does it echo Rita's life and upbringing?

Willy Russell: 'I wanted to make a play which engaged and was relevant to those who had no knowledge of literature, those who considered themselves uneducated, those whose daily language is not the language of the university or the theatre. In short I wanted to write a play which would attract and be as valid for the Ritas in the audience as the Franks.'

The plays in performance

It is important to remember that plays are written to be performed, not just to be read. This section helps you to see the plays as theatre and through rehearsing and improvising scenes to see their dramatic potential.

What the critics said

Educating Rita was first performed at the Warehouse Theatre in London in 1980.

Read this review which principally gives an account of the play and its themes.

▷ Do you think the writer shows a good understanding of the themes and issues raised in the play? Is there anything she says which you would disagree with? Do you think she gives a complete account of the play, or has she left anything out?

This brilliantly performed comedy centres upon the passionate desire of a young northern girl to attain a proper education in order to equip her for the higher echelons of a life to which she so longingly aspires. Her transformation from a culturally naive modern girl to a successful student is at once subtle and striking in Willy Russell's sharp and witty dialogue and Julie Walters' remarkable performance as Rita. From her first entrance into the study of her prospective tutor, who is to treat her to the delights of an Open University course, she rings true. She wanders wide-eyed around the study, touching the books and announcing that she wants an education, "a better culture". For Frank, the well-worn, quotation-battered intellectual, she is a refreshing change from the pretentious and take-it-or-leave-it attitude of the students he has been used to.

Rita works as a hairdresser and, in her mid-twenties, figures that there is more to life than 'creme' rinses and perms that go wrong. She wants to digest Chekhov and Shakespeare, Forster and Ibsen and she wants to pass exams. Frank's prime objective is to draw her away from the trashy paperbacks on which she has been reared and to teach her to appreciate and dissect the qualities of great literature. "How would you solve the problems of staging Peer Gynt?" is the title of one essay he sets her. For Rita, unaccustomed as she is to theorizing and churning out facts to please examiners, the answer is simple – "Do it on the radio". Besides coming to grips with the slow learning process, Rita has problems with her husband, whom she tries to convince that an individual has a right to choose. "He thinks we've got choice because he can go into a pub and choose between eight different lagers", and she ends up with, inevitably, a broken marriage but, eventually, an education. Frank, however, does not see this new-found knowledge as a change for the better and in the end there exists between them a relationship not dissimilar to the psychiatrist/patient relationship in *Equus*. He has cured Rita of her so-called ignorance but her passionate innocence has gone. He is left wondering where he will ever find such honesty again and we are left wondering whether Rita, now fully equipped for a better life crammed with opportunities, will find greater happiness. Mark Kingston's portrayal of Frank is a beautiful study of an academic for whom alcohol is an anaesthetic numbing the pain of his failed creativity, and Mike Ockrent's direction of the two performers is well-balanced in this thoroughly entertaining production.

(Rowena Kingman, *Drama*, October 1980)

▷ At what moment in the play do you think this picture was taken? What details suggest that the play is set in the late 1970s?

▷ At what moment in the play do you think this picture was taken?

The play was revived in New York in 1987.

▷ Read this review of the production. Do you think the play would transfer well to America? Can Americans understand our class differences?

Do you agree that 'the situation is contrived'? And that it is unwise to set the play in the present? Is it important that Rita has an authentic Liverpudlian accent? What impression of the production do you get from the review?

Mr. Pendleton plays the teacher as a fusty, effete academic who hides behind his books (and who seems to hide behind his shaggy corona of gray hair). Awakened by the aggressiveness of his pupil, he begins to put himself back in working order. In contrast to his predecessors in the role, Mr. Pendleton poses no real romantic challenge for Rita – and the possibility of a liaison should be in the air.

However, as the actor makes us realize, many different kinds of teachers can assume a role in the education of Rita. His is one specific approach, and, Mr. Pendleton is convincing (though he barely attempts an English accent). As a result, the play, which normally is centered around the student, shifts in the direction of the teacher; he becomes the audience's chief point of symphathy. Jeff Perry has given the play a compact production – "Educating Rita" profits from being on a small stage such as this one – although, in order to inject action into a basically static situation, the actors are asked to shift, needlessly, from chair to chair.

Many of Mr. Russell's lines are still amusing. At the same time, the situation is contrived. The play seems rooted in the 1970's, although, unwisely, the current production pretends to take place in the present. With its references to such people as Lawrence Ferlinghetti and Farrah Fawcett before she dropped the Majors, the "present" seems more than a decade at a remove. Today an uneducated Rita might bypass the open university system and start out as a fashion trendsetter. One thing has come full cycle: Rita's short skirts are back in vogue.

(Mel Gussow, *New York Times*, 8 May 1987)

Pygmalion was revived in London in 1984. There is a photograph of this production on the following page.

▷ Read these reviews of the production. How closely does Peter O'Toole fit your view of Professor Higgins? And Jackie Smith-Wood your view of Eliza?

I'd begun to think never again to see Pygmalion without missing the music.

We've grown so accustomed to the grown-up face of My Fair Lady that watching Shaw's original had become rather like catching a lady before she has quite finished her make-up and combed her hair.

Not that we have much time to dwell on this in the lavish revival from Mr Ray Cooney's latest Theatre of Comedy Company's production.

There is no room for music and Peter O'Toole on one stage in the confines of a three-act comedy. No need to wonder why this Professor Higgins is dreaded at polite tea parties.

Scarcely has he entered his mother's exquisite drawing room than he has kicked over the fire irons and is doing a deft juggling act with a delicate grandmother clock.

He then proceeds to loll all over the saintly Miss Joyce Carey (clearly resigned to paying the price of letting her son run wild in youth) or lope around the furniture like an Afghan puppy clearly anxious to go walkies.

Of course it's Shaw's fault. If he had not wanted to give an actor of Mr O'Toole's devilish invention his head, he should not have catalogued all Henry's faults so scrupulousy.

Shoes are pulled off and waved under the noses of visitors, feet scratched, hats flung over clocks, coats hurled under chairs.

Mercifully there is no chandelier, or Professor Higgins would undoubtedly have swung from it.

His constant prodding of poor Eliza might well have aroused her worst fears as to his intentions if we did not know this was only Mr O'Toole's way of signalling that he regarded her as no more than clay to be moulded.

The rest of the cast never once show signs of being blown off their true course by this tornado approach.

Jackie Smith-Wood is the most striking of Elizas. A spitfire street urchin who blossoms into a poised beauty without ever letting the light of battle die from her watchful eyes.

This transformation from flower-girl to Henry's equal is completed with all the dignity of soul Shaw could have wished.

There is a masterly rubicund Alfred Doolittle from John Thaw; an over-grown schoolboy Colonel Pickering from the benign Jack Watling; and a surprisingly human Mrs Eynsford Hill from Barbara Murray.

All in all Mr Cooney and company can continue to congratulate themselves on bringing a fresh look to familiar comedies. Certainly you will not see another Henry Higgins like this.

(*London Theatre Review*, 7–20 May, 1984)

Peter O'Toole as Professor Higgins and Jackie Smith-Wood as Eliza.

▷ Read the review of *Pygmalion* opposite. How do Paula Wilcox and Donald Pickering in the 1980 production compare with Jackie Smith-Wood and Peter O'Toole in their interpretation of the characters? Which do you think you would prefer?

The production was served by other enjoyable performances, particularly by the women. Paula Wilcox was a delight as Eliza, and made the transition from 'the squashed cabbage leaves of Covent Garden' to confident thoroughbred with apparent ease. Here is an actress who knows how to play comedy, to time a laugh line and reinforce it with a subtle expression (usually done under lowered eyelids). She made the famous small-talk scene at Mrs Higgins's at-home the funniest scene of the play. Sylvia Barter's Mrs Higgins was elegantly matriarchal, and had some well-played comic moments admonishing her somewhat doltish son. Rachel Thomas could have made Mrs Pearce a bit more indomitable, but she was still effective as Professor Higgins's housekeeper cum nanny.

Striding the stage in a well-cut brown suit, Donald Pickering played Professor Higgins as more an Edwardian dandy than the misogamist academic. He gave the role a sophistication that contrasted with the expected Rex Harrison permutation of the part, which could have been a valid interpretation. But he continually ran roughshod over his wittiest and most intelligent lines, making him seem a rather narcissistic, shallow creature as a result. He insisted on walking about, making pointless arcs around the furniture while speaking, only to return to his starting point. The scenes with Brian Oulton's Colonel Pickering seemed more like the immature pranks of schoolboys rather than the plans of two rather oblivious middle-aged bachelors.

(*Plays and Players*, May 1980)

Present a scene

Creating tension

In pairs, read this extract from *Educating Rita* and discuss the questions that follow.

Frank Look, how about a proper lunch?
  Rita Lunch? (*She leaps up, grabs the copy of 'Macbeth', the can of drink and the apple and goes to the door*) Christ – me customer. She only wanted a demi-wave – she'll come out looking like a friggin' muppet (*She comes back to the table*) Ey' Frank, listen – I was thinkin of goin' to the art gallery tomorrow. It's me half-day off. D' y' wanna come with me?
Frank (*smiling*) All right.
     Rita goes to the door.
Frank (*looking at her*) And – look, what are you doing on Saturday?
  Rita I work.
Frank Well, when you finish work.
  Rita Dunno.
Frank I want you to come over to the house.
  Rita Why?
Frank Julia's organized a few people to come round for dinner.
  Rita An' y' want me to come? Why?
Frank Why do you think?
  Rita I dunno.
Frank Because you might enjoy it.
  Rita Oh.
Frank Will you come?
  Rita If'y want.
Frank What do you want?
  Rita All right. I'll come.
Frank Will you bring Denny?
  Rita I don't know if he'll come.
Frank Well ask him.
  Rita (*puzzled*) All right.
Frank What's wrong?
  Rita What shall I wear?
     Black-out
     Rita goes out.

The lines are unusually short. What effect is Russell trying to create? What are the characters thinking? Who is initiating the conversation? At what pace (how fast or slow) do you think the dialogue should be moving? What do you think the characters should be doing during the dialogue? Where might they be looking? What expressions might be reflected in their faces?

▷ Learn the dialogue and rehearse it, making use of what you learnt in discussion. Show your work to others and ask them how successfully they think you have captured the mood.

Creating humour

Now read this extract:

Rita It's terrible these days, the money, isn't it? With the inflation an' that. You work for the ordinary university, don't y'? With the real students. The Open University's different, isn't it?

Frank It's supposed to embrace a more comprehensive studentship, yes.

Rita (*inspecting a bookcase*) Degrees for dishwashers.

Frank Would you – erm – would you like to sit down?

Rita No! Can I smoke? (*She goes to her bag and rummages in it*)

Frank Tobacco?

Rita Yeh. (*She half-laughs*) Was that a joke? (*She takes out a packet of cigarettes and a lighter*) Here – d' y' want one? (*She takes out two cigarettes and dumps the packet on the desk*)

Compare Frank's humour ('It's supposed to embrace a more comprehensive studentship, yes') with Rita's ('Degrees for dishwashers'). What do you think is the difference? How would you say each line? What tone would you use? How important is pace if you are trying to deliver a funny line?

▷ Learn the dialogue and rehearse. Present it to others for their comments.

Creating a contrast

In pairs read this extract from *Pygmalion* and discuss the questions that follow.

Mrs Higgins (*dismayed*) Henry! (*Scolding him*) What are you doing here today? It is my at-home day: you promised not to come. (*As he bends to kiss her, she takes his hat off, and presents it to him*).

Higgins Oh bother! (*He throws the hat down on the table*).

Mrs Higgins Go home at once.

Higgins (*kissing her*) I know, mother. I came on purpose.

Mrs Higgins But you mustn't. I'm serious, Henry. You offend all my friends: they stop coming whenever they meet you.

Higgins Nonsense! I know I have no small talk; but people don't mind. (*He sits on the settee*).

Mrs Higgins Oh! don't they? Small talk indeed! What about your large talk? Really,
             dear, you mustn't stay.
Higgins I must. I've a job for you. A phonetic job.
Mrs Higgins No use, dear. I'm sorry; but I can't get round your vowels; and though I
             like to get pretty postcards in your patent shorthand, I always have to
             read the copies in ordinary writing you so thoughtfully send me.
Higgins Well, this isn't a phonetic job.
Mrs Higgins You said it was.
Higgins Not your part of it. I've picked up a girl.
Mrs Higgins Does that mean that some girl has picked you up?
Higgins Not at all. I don't mean a love affair.
Mrs Higgins What a pity!
Higgins Why?
Mrs Higgins Well, you never fall in love with anyone under forty-five. When will you
             discover that there are some rather nice-looking young women about?
Higgins Oh, I can't be bothered with young women. My idea of a lovable woman is
         somebody as like you as possible. I shall never get into the way of seriously
         liking young women: some habits lie too deep to be changed. (*Rising
         abruptly and walking about, jingling his money and his keys in his trouser
         pockets*) Besides, they're all idiots.

The scene is most effective if there is a strong contrast
between the way Higgins behaves and speaks and the
way his mother does. What would you have Higgins do
to show that he does not belong in his mother's lady-
like drawing room? How does Mrs Higgins react to his
presence? How would you bring out the humour in this
scene?

▷ Learn the dialogue and practise it. Perform your
piece to others and ask for their comments.

Having an argument

Now read this extract.

Higgins Put out the lights, Eliza; and tell Mrs Pearce not to make coffee for me in the
         morning: I'll take tea. (*He goes out*).

         *Eliza tries to control herself and feel indifferent as she rises and walks across
         to the hearth to switch off the lights. By the time she gets there she is on the
         point of screaming. She sits down in Higgins' chair and holds on hard to the
         arms. Finally she gives way and flings herself furiously on the floor, raging.*

Higgins (*in despairing wrath outside*) What the devil have I done with my
         slippers? (*He appears at the door*).
Liza (*snatching up the slippers, and hurling them at him one after the other
      with all her force*) There are your slippers. And there. Take your slippers;
      and may you never have a day's luck with them!
Higgins (*astounded*) What on earth – ! (*He comes to her*). What's the matter? Get
         up. (*He pulls her up*). Anything wrong?

Liza (*breathless*) Nothing wrong – with you. I've won your bet for you, havn't I? That's enough for you. *I* don't matter, I suppose.

Higgins You won my bet! You! Presumptuous insect! *I* won it. What did you throw those slippers at me for?

Liza Because I wanted to smash your face. I'd like to kill you, you selfish brute. Why didn't you leave me where you picked me out of – in the gutter? You thank God it's all over, and that now you can throw me back again there, do you? (*She crisps her fingers frantically*).

Higgins (*looking at her in cool wonder*) The creature is nervous, after all.

Liza (*gives a suffocated scream of fury, and instinctively darts her nails at his face*)!!

Higgins (*catching her wrists*) Ah! would you? Claws in, you cat. How dare you shew your temper to me? Sit down and be quiet. (*He throws her roughly into the easy-chair*).

Liza (*crushed by superior strength and weight*) What's to become of me? What's to become of me?

Higgins How the devil do I know what's to become of you? What does it matter what becomes of you?

Liza You don't care. I know you don't care. You wouldn't care if I was dead. I'm nothing to you – not so much as them slippers.

Higgins (*thundering*) Those slippers.

Liza (*with bitter submission*) Those slippers. I didn't think it made any difference now.

Again what contrast should there be between Higgins' behaviour and Eliza's? How energetic should the scene be? At what speed should it be played?

▷ Learn the dialogue and practise it. Perform your piece to others and ask for their comments.

Improvise a scene

▷ In pairs, improvise the following scenes.

1 The scene in which Rita goes home after her first tutorial and tells Denny all about it. Read Act 1, Scene 1 to remind yourselves of what happened in the tutorial.

2 Rita tells Frank that Denny in a fit of jealousy burnt all her books and her essay. Read her account (Act 1, Scene 5) and improvise the scene between Rita and Denny.

3 After Eliza has stormed out of Higgins' house she visits his mother. Improvise the scene in which she arrives at Mrs Higgins' house and tells her what has happened. Read Act 4 and Act 5 at the point where Mrs Higgins tells Pickering and Higgins what Eliza said, and use what you have read in your improvisation.

▷ Choose one of the improvisations you have done, and write it up in the form of a play.

▷ Write about how you set about your improvisation, describing the character you were playing and how you came to finalise the dialogue. How successful do you think your work was in capturing the right character and mood?

Compare the plays with the films

Film has more resources than theatre although theatre has the advantage of the special relationship between the actor and the audience. If you can see either the film of *Pygmalion* or of *My Fair Lady* and the film of *Educating Rita*, you will learn a good deal about the plays by comparing the media, and by listing the differences between film and play. (*My Fair Lady* was written as a musical using Shaw's dialogue, but making alterations to the plot and, of course, adding songs.) Here are some questions to start you thinking.

▷ Willy Russell wrote a play for two actors in one location. Why was it felt necessary in the film to increase the number of actors and locations? What do you think the extra characters add to the play? What difference do you think the film ending makes? Does it make the story more romantic?

▷ Is the portrayal of Covent Garden romanticised in *My Fair Lady*? Do the additional scenes at Ascot and the Ball enhance the play? Do the songs emphasise Shaw's more serious points, or do they make the play more romantic? What do you think of the ending?

Write a theatre programme

▷ Write a theatre programme for a production of
either *Educating Rita* or *Pygmalion*. You should include:

a cover design;
a brief account of the playwright's life;
a summary of the plot of the play and its themes;
a gallery of the characters of the play saying a little
   about each;
notes on the social attitudes of the period;
a cast list;
a collage of the most important lines in the play.

Here are some questions and suggestions to guide you:

1 Will your cover design show a particular scene from
   the play? Or will it be an abstract design bringing out
   a theme? Or a drawing of one or two of the
   characters?

2 Select the basic facts about the playwright's life – you
   will only need to write a paragraph. What other plays
   has he written? What was he like as a person? What
   themes appear often in his plays?

3 Bear in mind that your plot summary must be
   accurate but easy to follow. Audiences have only
   about five minutes to absorb the information before
   the play starts. Will you keep the end of the play
   secret, or will you hint at it? What do you think is the
   most important point the play makes?

4 Find photographs of faces from newspapers and
   magazines which you think best fit the characters.
   Decide what are the most important characteristics of
   each character.

5 Use the information given on pages 4–11 to guide
   you in writing about the period. Select the most
   important points and write a couple of paragraphs.

6 Choose actors you know from television and theatre
   who you think would best suit the parts.

7 Choose about ten quotations which you find
   particularly important and arrange them on a page in
   whatever design pleases you. You may add artwork
   where you think it is helpful.

8 Present your programme as a booklet. The cover
   design will obviously be on the front page. Look at
   some theatre programmes and see how they compare
   with yours. How will you organise the rest of the
   information? How will you lay it out on the page?
   Will you break up the print with artwork?

Longman Study Texts

Longman Study Texts

Educating Rita – *Willy Russell*
ISBN 0 582 33182 X

Pygmalion – *Bernard Shaw*
ISBN 0 582 33097 1

This edition of the play includes a personal essay by Willy Russell, about his own education. In addition, extensive notes and an interesting introduction offer further help and ideas to the student reader.

This edition includes a personal essay by John Russell Brown, where he discusses the plays of Bernard Shaw. There is also an introduction to *Pygmalion*, notes on the play, suggestions for follow-up work and study questions.

A selection of novels and stories from Longman Imprint Books, Longman Study Texts and Modern Women Writers:

Longman Study Texts

July's People by Nadine Gordimer
The Cone-Gatherers by Robin Jenkins
Paradise Postponed by John Mortimer
Saint Joan by Bernard Shaw
The Devil's Disciple by Bernard Shaw
Arms and the Man by Bernard Shaw

Modern Women Writers

Hotel du Lac by Anita Brookner
My Brilliant Career by Miles Franklin
City of Illusions by Ursula Le Guin
Edith Jackson by Rosa Guy
The Albatross and other stories by Susan Hill
Heat and Dust by Ruth Prawer Jhabvala

Longman Imprint Books

P'tang, Yang, Kipperbang by Jack Rosenthal
John Mortimer Plays

Titles in the Longman Literature Guidelines series:

Animal Farm
The Diary of Anne Frank
An Inspector Calls
The Winslow Boy
Romeo and Juliet
Macbeth
I'm the King of the Castle
Educating Rita
Brave New World

Acknowledgements

We are grateful to the following for permission to reproduce copyright material:

Methuen London for extracts from *Educating Rita* and *Shirley Valentine* both by Willy Russell and the Society of Authors on behalf of the Bernard Shaw Estate for extracts from *Pygmalion*. (c) 1957, The Public Trustees as Executor of the Estate of Bernard Shaw.

Series designed by Jenny Portlock of Pentaprism.

We are grateful to the following for permission to reproduce photographs:

Barnaby's Picture Library, page 10 above (photo William Bowman), 11 (photo Adrian C. Muttitt); Camera Press, pages 10 below (photo Colin Davey) and 29 (Karsh of Ottawa); Dominic Photography, pages 15 above, 21, 27 (photos Zoe Dominic), 31, 33, 34 (photos Catherine Ashmore), 38 and 41 (photos Zoe Dominic); Ronald Grant Archives, pages 40, 44(2) and 45(2); John Haynes, page 36(2); Kobal Collection, pages 2 and 14; Mansell Collection, pages 4, 5 above, 6, 7 and 18; Mary Evans Picture Library, pages 5 below, 8, 9 above and 9 below (Fawcett Library); Rank Film Distributors and Acorn Pictures, pages 15 below, 24 and cover.

LONGMAN GROUP UK LIMITED,

Longman House, Burnt Mill, Harlow,
Essex CM20 2JE, England
and Associated Companies throughout the world.

First published 1990

Set in 10½/12½ pt Cheltenham Light and 10½/13 Helvetica
Produced by Longman Group (FE) Ltd
Printed in Hong Kong

ISBN 0 582 03894 4